Readalong

Here we go round the mulberry bush

A traditional song
illustrated by Pat Reynolds

Here we go round

the mulberry bush,

The mulberry bush,

the mulberry bush.

Here we go round
   the mulberry bush,
Early in the morning.

This is the way

    we wash our hands,

We wash our hands,

    we wash our hands.

This is the way
  we wash our hands,
Early in the morning.

Here we go round

the mulberry bush,

The mulberry bush,

the mulberry bush.

Here we go round

the mulberry bush,

Early in the morning.

This is the way
we brush our teeth,
We brush our teeth,
we brush our teeth.

This is the way
   we brush our teeth,
Early in the morning.

Here we go round

the mulberry bush,

The mulberry bush,

the mulberry bush.

Here we go round

the mulberry bush,

Early in the morning.

This is the way

     we comb our hair,

We comb our hair,

     we comb our hair.

This is the way

   we comb our hair,

Early in the morning.

Here we go round

the mulberry bush,

The mulberry bush,

the mulberry bush.

Here we go round

the mulberry bush,

Early in the morning.

This is the way

    we go to school,

We go to school,

    we go to school.

This is the way

    we go to school,

Early in the

    morning.